PIANO . VOCAL . GUITAR

TOP DOWNLOADS 2012

ISBN 978-1-4803-3795-4

7777 W. BLUEMOUND RD. P.O. BOX 13819 MILWAUKEE, WI 53213

Visit Hal Leonard Online at
www.halleonard.com

BEAUTY AND A BEAT

Words and Music by JUSTIN BIEBER,
NICKI MINAJ, MAX MARTIN,
ANTON ZASLAVSKI and SAVAN KOTECHA

Moderately fast

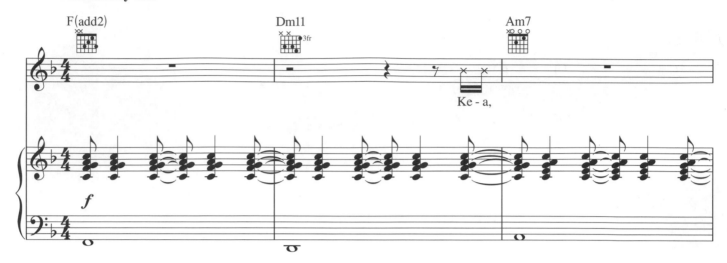

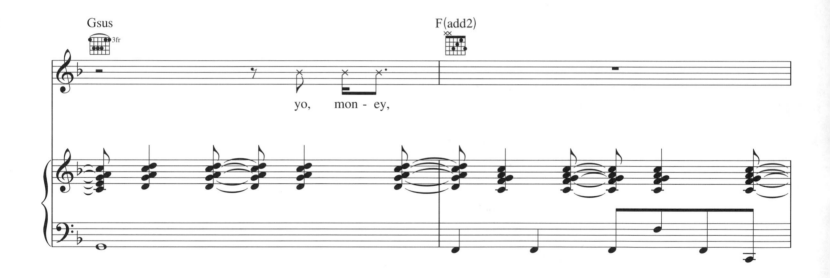

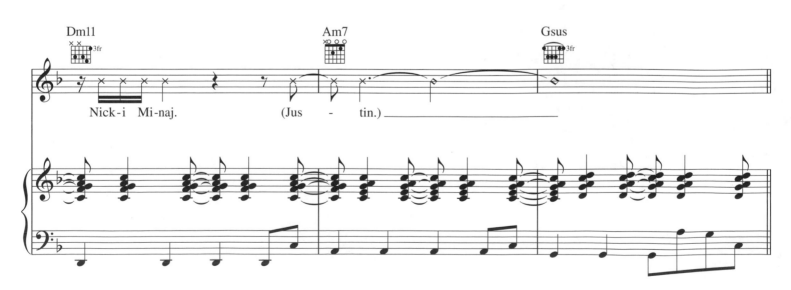

10

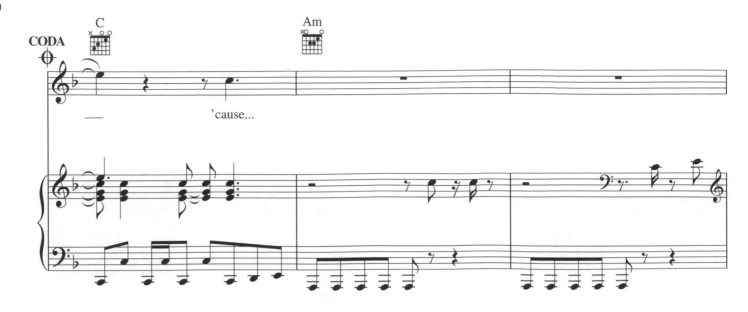

'cause...

Rap Lyrics

In time, ink lines, bitches couldn't get on my incline.
World tours, it's mine: ten little letters on a big sign.
Justin Bieber, you know I'm 'a hit 'em with the ether.
Buns out, wiener, but I gotta keep a eye out for Selena.

Beauty, beauty and the beat, beauty from the east, beautiful confessions of the priest.
Beats, beauty from the streets, we don't get deceased ev'ry time a beauty on the beats.
Beats... Yeah, yeah, yeah, yeah.
Let's go, let's go.

DIE YOUNG

Words and Music by KESHA SEBERT,
BENJAMIN LEVIN, LUKASZ GOTTWALD,
HENRY WALTER and NATE RUESS

Let's make the most of the night like we're gon - na die _____ young.

Young hearts, out our minds,
Young hunks tak - ing shots,

run - ning till we out of time. Wild childs, look - ing good,
strip - ping down to dirt - y socks. Mu - sic up, get - ting hot,

liv - ing hard just like we should. Don't care who's watch - ing when we
kiss me, give me all you got. It's pret - ty ob - vi - ous that

DIAMONDS

Words and Music by SIA FURLER,
TOR HERMANSEN, MIKKEL ERIKSEN
and BENJAMIN LEVIN

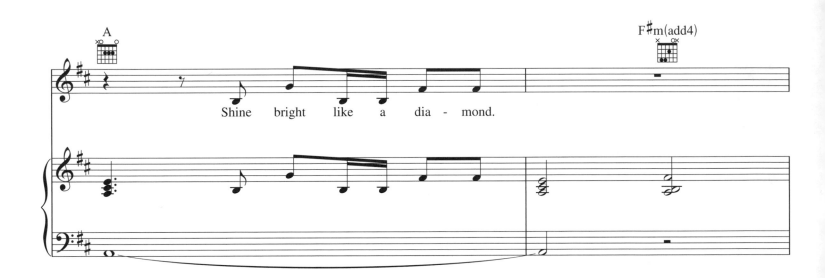

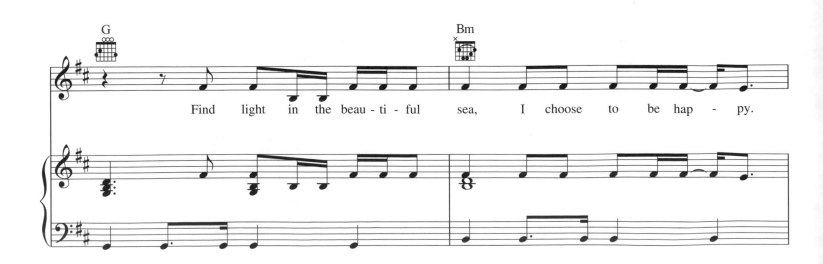

GANGNAM STYLE

Words and Music by GUN HYUNG YOO
and JAI SANG PARK

Techno Dance beat

Op - pan Gang-nam style   Gang-nam style

Rap 1: Na - je - neun ta - sa - ro-oon
Rap 2: *(See additional lyrics)*

Eh - eh - eh - eh - eh - eh   Op - pan Gang-nam style   Ah

Additional Lyrics

2. Jeong-sook-kae bo-i-ji-man nol taen no-neun yeo-ja
   I-tae-da shi-peu-myeon mook-eot-teon meo-ri poo-neun yeo-ja
   Ga-ryeot-ji-man wen-man-han no-chool-bo-da ya-han yeo-ja
   Geu-reon gam-gak-jeo-gin yeo-ja
   Na-neun sa-na-i
   Jeom-ja-na bo-i-ji-man nol taen no-neun sa-na-i
   Tae-ga dwe-myeon wan-jeon mi-chyeo-beo-ri-neun sa-na-i
   Geun-yook-bo-da sa-sang-i ool-toong-bool-toong-han sa-na-i
   Geu-reon sa-na-i
   Chorus

English Translation

Intro: Oppa lives a Gangnam style life
         Gangnam style

1. (I love) a lady who is warm and compassionate by the day
   A classy lady who can afford a relaxing cup of coffee
   But whose heart starts burning when the night comes
   A lady who has such a twisted charm
   I'm a guy
   A guy who is as warm as you by the day
   A guy who downs the boiling hot coffee in one go
   A guy whose heart starts exploding when the night comes
   I'm that kind of guy

Chorus: Beautiful, lovely, yes you are, hey, yes you are, hey
         Beautiful, lovely, yes you are, hey, yes you are, hey
         Shall we go all the way from now on?
         Oppa lives a Gangnam style life
         Eh, sexy lady, oppa lives a Gangnam style life

2. (I love) a virtuous lady who can have a ball
   A lady who undoes her ponytail when the time comes
   And who's sexy even without wearing skimpy clothes
   Such a sensuous lady
   I'm a guy
   A guy who goes completely crazy when the time comes
   And whose ideas are bumpier than his muscles
   I'm that kind of guy
   Chorus

Bridge: Over a running guy, there's a flying guy
         Baby, baby, I'm kind of a know-it-all
         You know what I'm sayin'?
         Oppa lives a Gangnam style life
         Eh, sexy lady, oppa lives a Gangnam style life

HOME

Words and Music by GREG HOLDEN
and DREW PEARSON

GOOD TIME

Words and Music by ADAM YOUNG,
MATTHEW THIESSEN and BRIAN LEE

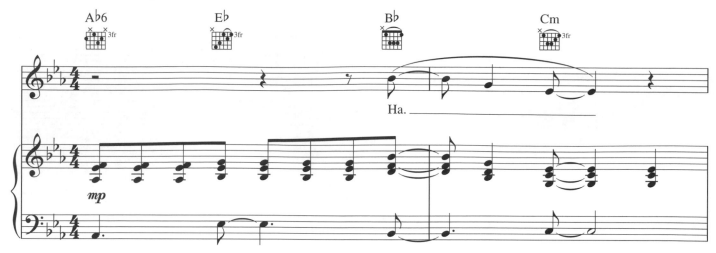

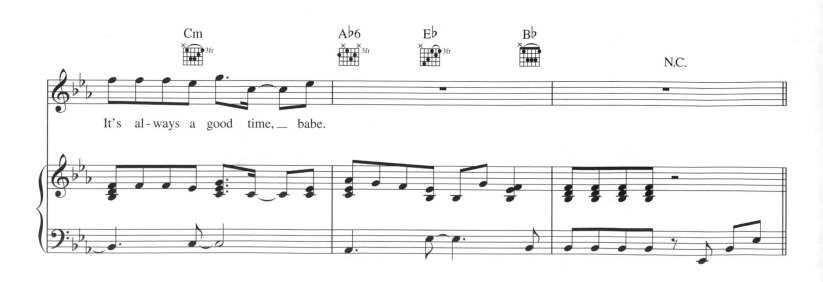

LIVE WHILE WE'RE YOUNG

Words and Music by RAMI YACOUB,
SAVAN KOTECHA and CARL FALK

ONE MORE NIGHT

Words and Music by ADAM LEVINE,
JOHAN SCHUSTER and MAX MARTIN

SET FIRE TO THE RAIN

Words and Music by ADELE ADKINS
and FRASER SMITH

WHEN I WAS YOUR MAN

Words and Music by BRUNO MARS,
ARI LEVINE, PHILIP LAWRENCE
and ANDREW WYATT

Moderately

Same bed, but it feels just a lit-tle bit big-
My pride, my __ e-go, my needs and my self-

- ger now.
- ish ways

Our song on the ra-di-o, but it don't sound __
caused a good strong __ wo-man like you to walk out __

__ the same.
__ my life.

When our friends talk a-bout you, all it does is just tear __
Now I __ nev-er get to clean up the mess __

SOME NIGHTS

Words and Music by JEFF BHASKER,
ANDREW DOST, JACK ANTONOFF
and NATE RUESS

Moderately, with a March feel

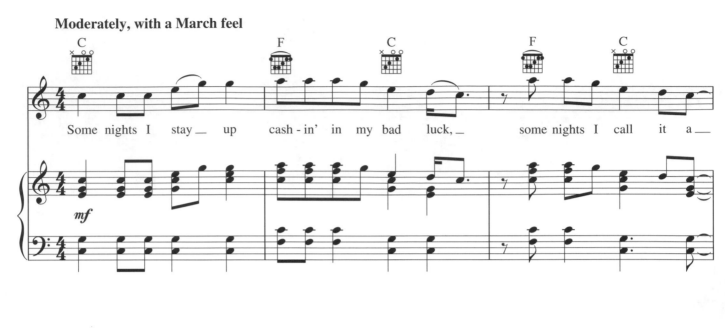

Some nights I stay __ up cash-in' in my bad luck, __ some nights I call it a __

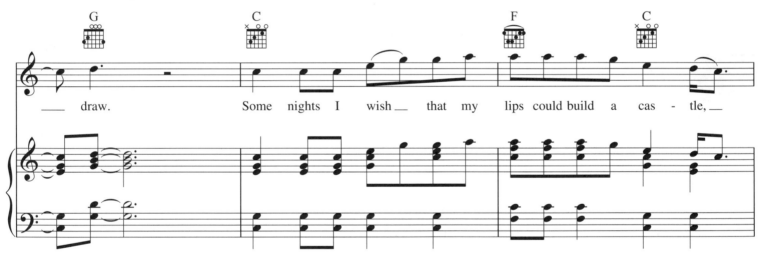

__ draw. Some nights I wish __ that my lips could build a cas - tle, __

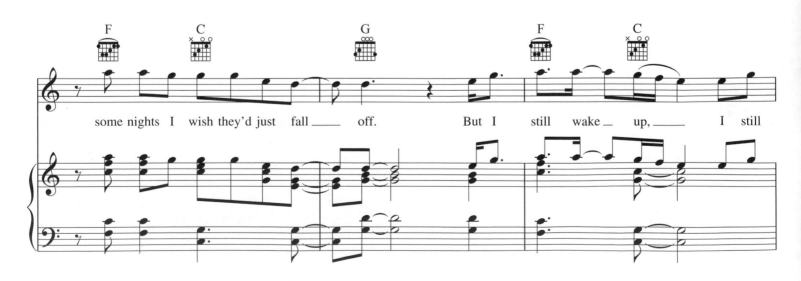

some nights I wish they'd just fall __ off. But I still wake __ up, __ I still

TRY

Words and Music by busbee
and BEN WEST

WE ARE NEVER EVER GETTING BACK TOGETHER

Words and Music by TAYLOR SWIFT,
SHELLBACK and MAX MARTIN

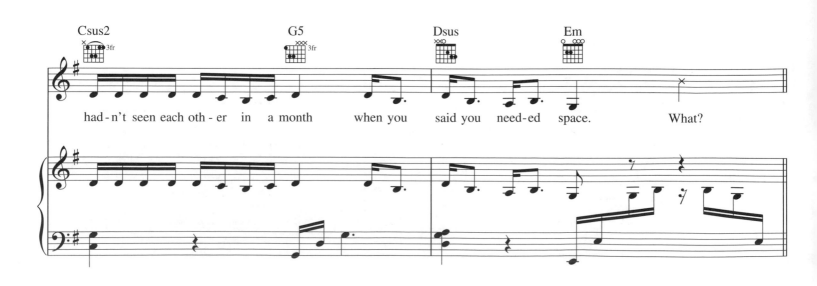

WE ARE YOUNG

Words and Music by JEFF BHASKER,
ANDREW DOST, JACK ANTONOFF
and NATE RUESS

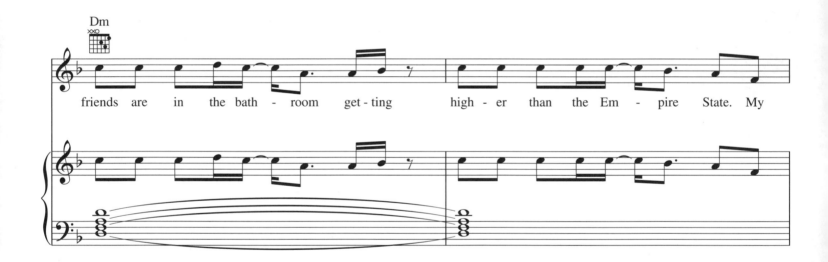

WHISTLE

Words and Music by TRAMAR DILLARD,
DAVID EDWARD GLASS, JUSTIN FRANKS,
ANTONIO MOBLEY, BREYAN ISAAC
and MARCUS KILLIAN

Moderately fast

(Whistle)

Can you blow my whis-tle, ba-by, whis-tle, ba-by?

Let me know. Girl, I'm gon-na show you how to do it, and we start real slow. You just

Let your lips spin back a-round cor - ner. Slow it down, ba - by, take a lit - tle long - er.
Can you blow my

D.S. al Coda

CODA

It's like

ev -'ry - where I go, my whis-tle read - y to blow. Shaw - ty don't e - ven know she can get an - y - bod - y low. Per-

(Whistle)

Go on, girl, you can twerk it, let me see you whis-tle while you work it. I'm a lay back, don't stop it, 'cause I love it how you drop it, drop it, drop it on me.

WIDE AWAKE

Words and Music by KATY PERRY,
LUKASZ GOTTWALD, MAX MARTIN,
HENRY WALTER and BONNIE McKEE